Ancient Civilizations of Central and South America

An Enthralling Introduction to the Olmecs, Maya, Toltecs, Aztecs, and Incas

© Copyright 2022

All Rights Reserved. No part of this book may be reproduced in any form without permission in writing from the author. Reviewers may quote brief passages in reviews.

Disclaimer: No part of this publication may be reproduced or transmitted in any form or by any means, mechanical or electronic, including photocopying or recording, or by any information storage and retrieval system, or transmitted by email without permission in writing from the publisher.

While all attempts have been made to verify the information provided in this publication, neither the author nor the publisher assumes any responsibility for errors, omissions or contrary interpretations of the subject matter herein.

This book is for entertainment purposes only. The views expressed are those of the author alone, and should not be taken as expert instruction or commands. The reader is responsible for his or her own actions.

Adherence to all applicable laws and regulations, including international, federal, state and local laws governing professional licensing, business practices, advertising and all other aspects of doing business in the US, Canada, UK or any other jurisdiction is the sole responsibility of the purchaser or reader.

Neither the author nor the publisher assumes any responsibility or liability whatsoever on the behalf of the purchaser or reader of these materials. Any perceived slight of any individual or organization is purely unintentional.

Free limited time bonus

Stop for a moment. We have a free bonus set up for you. The problem is this: we forget 90% of everything that we read after 7 days. Crazy fact, right? Here's the solution: we've created a printable, 1-page pdf summary for this book that you're reading now. All you have to do to get your free pdf summary is to go to the following website: **https://livetolearn.lpages.co/enthrallinghistory/**

Once you do, it will be intuitive. Enjoy, and thank you!

Contents

INTRODUCTION 1
CHAPTER 1: THE OUTSTANDING OLMECS 3
CHAPTER 2: THE MARVELOUS MAYA 12
CHAPTER 3: THE TERRIFIC TOLTECS 26
CHAPTER 4: THE AMAZING AZTECS 35
CHAPTER 5: THE INCREDIBLE INCAS 44
CONCLUSION 54
HERE'S ANOTHER BOOK BY ENTHRALLING HISTORY THAT YOU MIGHT LIKE 56
FREE LIMITED TIME BONUS 57
BIBLIOGRAPHY 58

Introduction

When people talk about Native Americans or Indigenous Americans, their thoughts often go to the native peoples who live in what is now the United States and Canada. Unfortunately, this means that several important tribes from Mexico and other countries in Central and South America often go undiscussed. This short guide seeks to remedy this.

This book will discuss five of the most impressive tribes and civilizations from ancient Central and South America: the Olmecs, Maya, Toltecs, Aztecs, and Incas. Most history guides leave out the Olmecs and Toltecs since less is known about these people groups than the others. Of course, that doesn't make these two civilizations any less impressive.

Each of these civilizations has similarities, but they also have things that help them to stand out and distinguish themselves from one another. While it would be easy to lump all of these civilizations into one general "Middle American Indigenous people" group, that would not do their individual accomplishments justice. Some of the biggest differences between these groups include their architectural styles, metalwork, religions, farming practices, and trading.

It is also important to note that while some of these civilizations were active at the same time, others are separated by hundreds of years! Because of this, the timelines of these cultures may not line up with each other. The collective civilizations are not discussed in chronological order, but we will discuss the events of each individual civilization (within their respective chapter) in chronological order. Most of the civilizations came to an end or petered out around the time when Spanish conquistadors arrived in the Americas, although some seemed to have disappeared without a trace!

Throughout this book, we will look at some of these civilizations' greatest accomplishments and general culture. We will go as far back to the beginning as we can until when the civilization disappeared or assimilated into other cultures. We will also take a look at the cultural practices that are still used and how the descendants of these cultures see themselves today.

Although not all of these civilizations had customs that trickled down to us today, there is no doubt that they impacted the history of Mexico and other countries. Now, let's take a cursory dive into each of these five amazing civilizations to learn more about them!

Chapter 1: The Outstanding Olmecs

The Olmec civilization sprang up around what is now the present-day Gulf of Mexico in about 1200 BCE. We know this because the Olmecs founded their first major city (and capital), San Lorenzo, around this time. However, this name is Spanish; the Olmecs would have called the city something else. Over time, other Olmec cities appeared. The civilization flourished for about eight hundred years. However, in about 900 BCE, San Lorenzo was destroyed. The Olmecs then moved their capital to La Venta (which again would have had a different name). This city was destroyed sometime between 300 and 400 BCE. Shortly afterward, the Olmec civilization declined and came to an end.[1] Oddly enough, historians still do not know what exactly caused the Olmec civilization's end. Unlike many of the other civilizations in this book, they were not conquered by the Spanish. Instead, it is likely that a variety of factors, such as drought and war, could have slowly led to the civilization's decline.

---

[1] World History Encyclopedia. "Olmec Civilization Timeline." World History Encyclopedia RSS,
2022. https://www.worldhistory.org/timeline/Olmec_Civilization/

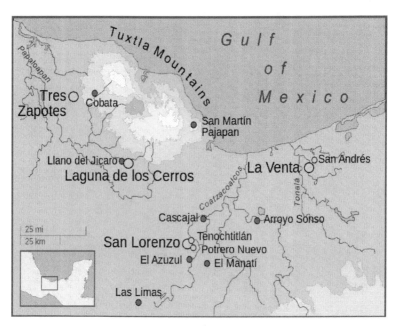

Map of the Olmec heartland.
CC-BY-4.0 https://creativecommons.org/licenses/by/4.0 via Wikimedia Commons: https://commons.wikimedia.org/wiki/File:Olmec_Heartland_Overview_4.svg

Architecture

Unlike the Maya, Aztec, and Inca civilizations, not much of the Olmec architecture survived. This is, in part, because a great percentage of their "permanent" buildings were in San Lorenzo and La Venta, which are now destroyed. Because of this, historians need to make educated guesses on what the Olmecs' architecture was like based on the few remaining ruins and artwork that still remains today.

Like many Mesoamerican civilizations, the Olmecs built pyramids or ziggurats. These were similar to the famous Egyptian pyramids, but they were terraced. They looked like they were one large triangle made of stairs. Like Egyptian pyramids, these ziggurats were used for religious or ceremonial purposes. It is also possible that Olmec royalty, government officials, priests, and other rich or influential community members would use these structures.[2] Many of these

---

[2] Scheper, George L. "The Olmec World." Academia.edu. Academia, October 1, 2014.

educated guesses are based on how other Mesoamerican civilizations and the Egyptians used their pyramids and ziggurats.

The remaining Olmec structures are made out of local stones. There are a few reasons for this. The first reason is that both the cities of La Venta and San Lorenzo are near natural rock formations. This would have given the Olmecs easy access to large chunks of stone without needing to travel far or mine deep underground.[3] The Olmecs may have used other materials, but wood and other biodegradable materials would have rotted away by the time historians discovered the Olmec sites. This would have happened quickly due to Mexico's humidity and generally wet weather.

Another outstanding feature of Olmec architecture is the use of stone columns. These were often made of sandstone or basalt, which were both local stones. Columns were used rarely, mostly in tombs, temples, and other ceremonial buildings. These columns would sometimes be carved with ornate patterns. Historians suspect these columns were made to look like or represent trees.[4] Many of the finer engravings have since eroded. Luckily, deeper carved lines have retained their shapes, for the most part, giving historians a glimpse into the past.

Culture and Daily Life

Like many other civilizations throughout the Americas, the Olmecs mostly survived by a combination of farming, hunting, gathering, and trading. Gender roles, for the most part, determined which people would do which tasks. Women usually stayed near the home to raise the children and cook. Men were the hunters and traders. Both men and women would take part in farming and make artwork, such as pottery and weaving.[5] Like most other American civilizations at the

---

https://www.academia.edu/8578552/The_Olmec_World_or_the_Formative_Era_Ceremonial_Complex_DrafText_Copy_2.
[3] Scheper, 2014.
[4] Scheper, 2014.
[5] Minster, Christopher. "Ancient Olmec Culture." ThoughtCo, May 30, 2019.

time, the Olmecs' staple foods were squash, beans, and maize (corn). They would have farmed similar to how it is done today—minus the machines and chemicals.

The Olmecs lived similarly to those in the Stone Age, as they mostly used tools made of various stones, clay, and bones. Some of the basic tools the Olmecs would have made and used included mortars, hammers, knives, spearheads, arrows, and pots. Sometimes, the Olmecs would make items out of obsidian, an extremely sharp rock. However, obsidian was not native to the Olmec homelands, so this was a material they would have had to trade for with neighboring civilizations.[6] It is not known how much items like obsidian or pottery were worth, as they did not trade for money; instead, they traded for other goods. However, it is likely that the common people would not have had access to obsidian or other expensive minerals, like gold and gems.

It is also important to remember that the Olmec civilization began sometime around 1200 BCE. This is considerably earlier than many of the other ancient Mesoamerican civilizations. Because of this, they would not have had much influence from other cultures. However, the Olmecs would go on to heavily influence the other civilizations around them until their decline in about 400 BCE.

San Lorenzo and La Venta

San Lorenzo is in the modern-day state of Veracruz. The settlement had been occupied since about 1500 BCE by several other civilizations before the Olmecs made their claim on the land. These include the Ojochi, Bajío, and Chicharras. However, the city did not reach its peak until a couple of hundred years into the Olmec occupation, from about 1150 to 900 BCE. At its height, the city could

---

https://www.thoughtco.com/olmec-culture-overview-2136299 (accessed May 17, 2022).
[6] Minster, Christopher. "Ancient Olmec Culture."

have held around thirteen thousand inhabitants.[7] Because of this, readers may see this city referred to as the first Olmec capital.

Olmec ruins.

Xeas23, CC BY-SA 3.0 https://creativecommons.org/licenses/by-sa/3.0 via Wikimedia Commons: https://commons.wikimedia.org/wiki/File:FUERTE_SAN_LORENZO_2.JPG

Today, little remains of San Lorenzo. Due to general cultural decline and the humid climate, many of the old stone buildings in the area have been desecrated or eroded. All wooden buildings have disappeared. Some of the most important structures that remain are the royal compound and the red palace. The city also has some of Mexico's earliest aqueducts.[8] These aqueducts and other buildings were likely either independently invented by the Olmecs or based on the architecture of previous civilizations in this part of Mexico.

San Lorenzo began to decline in population around 900 BCE, around the same time as the rise of La Venta. No one really knows why the city began to decline so shortly after its peak. However, some

---

[7] Minster, Christopher. "The Historic Olmec City of San Lorenzo." ThoughtCo, June 15, 2019. https://www.thoughtco.com/the-olmec-city-of-san-lorenzo-2136302 (accessed May 17, 2022).
[8] Minster, Christopher. "The Historic Olmec City of San Lorenzo."

scientists theorize that climate change, which could have impacted farming and hunting, may have had something to do with it.[9]

La Venta was originally on an island near the Tonalá River, near modern-day Veracruz. This city was created around 800 BCE, shortly after the fall of San Lorenzo. One thing that makes this city stand out to modern-day researchers is the Great Mound. This is a large pyramid-like heap of earth, akin to a manmade hill. Historians guess that the Great Mound was used for ceremonial or religious purposes. The mound and much of the surrounding area in La Venta were surrounded by large stone walls or fences. Archaeologists have also found several tombs in the city, many of which were filled with offerings to the dead or gods. La Venta is a popular tourist destination today because of the many large stone Olmec heads in the city.[10] Since La Venta was not occupied for as long as San Lorenzo, much less is known about this city. However, since it was occupied *later* than San Lorenzo, more high-quality artifacts and artworks have survived from this site.

Religious Beliefs

Surprisingly, historians know a lot about the Olmec religion and gods. The Olmec people were polytheistic, meaning they worshiped more than one god or goddess. Historians know about at least eight Olmec gods. Oddly enough, many of these gods did not have a gender; instead, they were androgynous. Historians figured this out through surviving Olmec artwork.[11] The Olmecs did have a written language (similar to Egyptian hieroglyphics), but historians cannot yet read it. Some of their language has been deciphered, but not all of it.

---

[9] Minster, Christopher. "The Historic Olmec City of San Lorenzo."
[10] "Early Classic Period (100–600 CE)." Encyclopedia Britannica. Encyclopedia Britannica, inc. Accessed May 18, 2022. https://www.britannica.com/topic/pre-Columbian-civilizations/Early-Classic-period-100-600-ce.
[11] "The Olmec | Ancient Civilizations (Article)." Khan Academy. Khan Academy, 2017. https://www.khanacademy.org/humanities/world-history/world-history-beginnings/ancient-americas/a/the-olmec article.

For this reason, historians can get the gist of what a passage says but not the exact meaning.[12] Even though some of the Olmec language can be deciphered, archaeologists have not been able to find anything written about the Olmec gods.[13] It is not known why the Olmecs did not write about their gods. It is possible that they spread their myths through oral tradition.

Most of the Olmec gods represented a specific purpose. For example, they had a maize god, a rain spirit, and a god that controlled fishing and the waters. Shamans and other religious leaders would perform religious rites and ceremonies. It is also likely that the classic Maya hoop ball game was first created (although perhaps in an altered form) by the Olmecs.[14] Other Mesoamerican civilizations had similar gods and religious ceremonies. While it is likely that they took a lot from the Olmec religion, it is also possible that their gods and rites were independently invented.

Art

Probably the most famous pieces of Olmec art are the Olmec heads. These sculptures, usually giant in size, were carved from one large stone. Sometimes, the stone had to be carried long distances to be carved and placed in a spot of honor. However, historians do not know how the heads or stones were transported. The first Olmec heads date back to the decline of San Lorenzo.[15] Because the Olmec heads were first made near the decline of San Lorenzo, there are many more heads in the La Venta ruins. As expected, the newer the sculptures are, the better shape they tend to be in.

---

[12] Heath, Haiden. "Has the Olmec Language Been Deciphered?" Rampfesthudson.com. Rampfest Hudson, October 25, 2019. https://www.rampfesthudson.com/has-the-olmec-language-been-deciphered/.
[13] "The Olmec | Ancient Civilizations (Article)." Khan Academy.
[14] "The Olmec | Ancient Civilizations (Article)." Khan Academy.
[15] "The Olmec | Ancient Civilizations (Article)." Khan Academy.

Giant Olmec head.
SMU Central University Libraries, No restrictions, via Wikimedia Commons: https://commons.wikimedia.org/wiki/File:Xalapa_Museum,_Veracruz,_La_Venta,_Olmec_(14038749787).jpg

Giant heads were not the only art the Olmec made. They also made other sculptures of stone, usually basalt. These could be three-dimensional sculptures or reliefs. Most of their sculptures depicted the gods or nature. The Olmecs also made pottery, jade jewelry, and various greenstone items.[16] Many of these artworks still survive in museums.

Decline

No one knows why the Olmec civilization began to decline after being prosperous for so long. Many historians theorize the decline had something to do with climate change or natural disasters. These would have contaminated or otherwise changed the water in such a

---

[16] "The Olmec | Ancient Civilizations (Article)." Khan Academy.

way that it could not be used for farming. Volcanoes were also active around this time (400 BCE), which would have made the land inhospitable.[17] With all of these changes, the Olmec people would have had to either move to new areas, likely dispersing in the process, or they would have starved to death.

Influence

The Olmecs are one of the oldest major Mesoamerican cultures. Other Mesoamerican civilizations both learned from and took from the Olmec culture and assimilated it into their own. At the same time, the Olmec themselves had little to take or learn from other cultures, making them more independent than most ancient cultures, both in Mesoamerica and around the world![18] Historians still have a lot to learn about the Olmecs. Once they make more discoveries and better understand the Olmec written language, they are sure to know more about other civilizations in Mexico as well.

---

[17] "The Olmec | Ancient Civilizations (Article)." Khan Academy.
[18] Minster, Christopher. "Ancient Olmec Culture."

Chapter 2: The Marvelous Maya

The Maya civilization is arguably one of the most influential of all the pre-Columbian Mexican cultures. The Maya borrowed from other civilizations while also having their own accomplishments and unique daily rituals, religious rites, and more.

    Each period in the Maya timeline is characterized by different accomplishments. The Preclassical period (1800 BCE-250 CE) is the first and longest period. The Maya civilization began forming a little earlier than the Olmecs. However, the civilizations grew up alongside each other, which is part of the reason they share so many commonalities. The Preclassical period is characterized by the Maya's first large-scale building projects, such as temples and ziggurats. The Maya also developed their writing system, a type of hieroglyphics, during this time period.[19] However, it should be noted that historians cannot fully understand Maya writing. Like Olmec writing, historians can only get the gist of what is written.

---

[19] VanVoorst, Jenny Fretland. *The Ancient Maya*. North Mankato, MN: Compass Point Books, 2013, 11.

Maya hieroglyphics.
https://pixabay.com/photos/palenque-museum-Maya-glyphs-1315851/

The Classic period took place between 250 and 900 CE. During this time, many Maya cities reached their peak. Advancements in architecture and other technologies freed up more time for the common people, which led to an intellectual boom. The Maya learned about math and astrology, and they spent much of their time following intricate religious rituals.

The Postclassic period began around 900 CE and ended with the fall of the Maya civilization in the 1500s. Before the Spanish came into Maya territory, the Maya focused less on their gods and more on a new god—money.[20] The arrival of the Spanish only amplified the Maya's urge to focus on their economy. They worked alongside the Spanish conquistadors (sometimes willingly and sometimes not) and traded gold and other resources for what the Spanish had to offer. The disease, warfare, and other issues brought on by the Spaniards' arrival would lead to the decline and destruction of the Maya in the 1500s.

---

[20] VanVoorst, Jenny Fretland. *The Ancient Maya*, 11.

Trade, Merchants, and Markets

The Maya didn't use money, at least in regards to the coins and/or paper money that we use today. Instead, they relied on trade and barter systems. The Maya could trade within their civilization or use the extensive trade routes that ran through Mexico and other areas of Mesoamerica. Some trade routes would be over two hundred miles long! Some expensive or "prized" trade items would have included luxury goods like gold, copper, jade, and other decorative items. These would be used to make jewelry, ceremonial items, and other expensive goods, but the gold and jewels themselves were never used as currency. More common trading items were food, pottery, and stone tools. These were less pricey, so they were traded more often than the expensive goods.

The trade routes expanded during the middle of the Preclassical period and continued to the decline of the Maya civilization.[21] Since historians do not yet understand Maya writing, we know little about the intricacies of the Maya economy. We do not know if anyone could use trade routes or if they were delegated to only the merchants. We also do not know how the trade routes were affected when the civilization declined; we only know that they *did* decline.

Politics

Most people will think of the Maya civilization as one unified country. However, the civilization could be compared to well-connected European city-states. Each city-state could dictate local laws and trade rules. At the same time, the Maya society as a whole had relationships and alliances with each other. This not only helped with trade but also with fighting; local city-states would often "team up" with each other to fight warring civilizations and tribes. There were

---

[21] Minster, Christopher. "Economy and Trade of the Ancient Mayas." ThoughtCo, April 24, 2021.
https://www.thoughtco.com/ancient-maya-economy-and-trade-2136168 (accessed May 18, 2022).

about twenty Maya city-states in total.[22] We know more about the Maya political structure, not so much because of their written records but because of the Spanish records.

For most of the Maya civilization, the population was ruled by government officials (*batabs*, *tupiles*, *ah cuch cabob*, and *halach uinic*), military leaders (*nacom*), and religious leaders (high priests). The government officials took care of all things regarding the general population, the religious leaders worked to keep the religious rites in order, and the military leaders commanded battles. Most of these leaders had others working under them to help keep the peace. The government undertakings were usually done locally; it seems the Maya did not have "federal" rules and laws. Law-breakers would be dealt with on a local level.[23] Many city-states would have had similar laws. The laws may have been agreed upon by councils. Councils from different city-states could have created some laws based on their alliances with each other.

Criminals did not get off easy when they committed crimes. Some common crimes included adultery, arson, murder, theft, assault, and breaking religious norms. Punishments could include anything from being publicly shamed to being executed or enslaved. Both men and women could be punished under Maya law. Criminals could also request pardons.[24] We do not know if children could be considered criminals. Historians also do not know all of the religious offenses that were punishable by law.

---

[22] "Maya Political Structure." Tarlton Law Library. The University of Texas at Austin, November 8, 2018. https://tarlton.law.utexas.edu/aztec-and-maya-law/maya-political-structure.
[23] "Maya Political Structure." Tarlton Law Library.
[24] "Maya Criminal Law." Tarlton Law Library. The University of Texas at Austin, November 8, 2018. https://tarlton.law.utexas.edu/aztec-and-maya-law/maya-criminal-law.

Religion

The Maya were very religious, especially during the Preclassical and Classic periods. They believed that there were three realms and that they believed that the Earth was in the middle. The place of the gods was in the sky, and the underworld lay beneath the waves; these were similar to the concepts of Hades and Mount Olympus in ancient Greece. In order to keep the gods happy, they would need to maintain order and balance on Earth.[25] This balance would be held by the people following both earthly laws and religious rules. Punishing criminals and religious offenders who broke these rules would help to restore balance. Performing religious ceremonies could accomplish the same goal.

The Maya were polytheistic people. They had one main "creator" god named Itzamná, sometimes also known as Hunab Ku. His wife was Ixchel, who was the goddess of childbirth, healing, and crafts. Other notable gods include Yum Cimil, the god of the underworld and death, and Yum Kaax, the agriculture and rain god. Most gods had their heavenly form but could also transform into a human or animal.[26] Again, readers can draw some comparisons from the Maya pantheon to the Greek and Roman gods. Like the Greek gods, Maya gods were flawed and complex characters. This seems to be a common pattern in polytheistic religions.

People who lived "good" lives would go to a heaven-like place, where they would have a peaceful and restful afterlife. People who lived "bad" lives would go to somewhere known as the "Place of Fear." Here, they would suffer everlasting torment. The Maya believed that both these heaven and hell-like places were real places but were invisible to living humans. The dead would be brought to heaven in the sky or brought to the hell-like place via underground caves on Earth. Following laws and religious rules, as well as performing religious rituals and sacrifices, could appease the gods.

---

[25] VanVoorst, Jenny Fretland. *The Ancient Maya*, 12–13.
[26] VanVoorst, Jenny Fretland. *The Ancient Maya*, 13–14.

Religious offerings could include anything from meat, precious gemstones (usually jade), and even blood and human sacrifices.[27]

It is impossible to say how many people were sacrificed. The numbers were likely exaggerated by the Spanish, who would have been horrified by the rituals. Because of the shock factor, the Spanish may have written about human sacrifices more than sacrifices involving meat and other items. It is likely that non-human sacrifices were made more often.

Daily Life in Different Social Classes

The Maya had different social classes, similar to India's caste system. A person's social status would dictate what kinds of things they would have to do and what they would be *allowed* to do on a daily basis.

Royalty, government officials, and other "higher-ups" would live lavish lifestyles, own expensive jeweled and gold items, wear fine clothing, and eat the best food. They may have had slaves or servants. They would rarely need to go outdoors or do any manual labor.[28] The "middle class" would have included warriors, scribes, and artisans. Not much is known about these people, likely because they spent much of their time either fighting or creating art and writing about the castes above them.[29] Like in most societies, the upper class contained the least amount of people who had the most wealth. The "middle class" was also fairly small and was much different than how we think of the middle class today.

The commoner class was the largest class. This class included farmers and general laborers. Farmers arguably worked the hardest and earned the least. They had to give about two-thirds of their harvest to the upper class, possibly as a form of taxation. Women, for the most part, stayed at home to take care of the children, make food, clean the home, and make basic clay pottery, woven baskets, and

---

[27] VanVoorst, Jenny Fretland. *The Ancient Maya*, 13–17.
[28] VanVoorst, Jenny Fretland. *The Ancient Maya*, 28–29.
[29] VanVoorst, Jenny Fretland. *The Ancient Maya*, 31.

plain clothing.[30] It was not likely that a commoner could "work their way up" to join a higher caste. For the most part, a person would stay in the class that they were born into for their whole lives.

The slaves were at the bottom of the class structure. People could either be born into slavery or become slaves if they were captured during wars or if they were criminals. Slaves could work in their master's home or be sent to do manual labor in mining operations or building projects. If a slave worked for a master, they would not be set free when their master died. Instead, they might be killed and buried with their master. They were expected to serve their master in the afterlife.[31] The Maya did not discriminate against their slaves based on race. Maya could have Maya slaves or slaves from other neighboring civilizations. It is unclear how much a slave would cost.

Maya Architecture

There are several famous Maya archaeological sites in Mexico—certainly too many to fit in this short guide. Below is a quick rundown of three of the most popular sites: Palenque, Tikal, and Chichén Itzá. Each of these sites has its own unique architecture and city layout.

Historians believe that people first began inhabiting Palenque around 100 BCE during the Preclassical period. It was abandoned around 900 CE at the start of the Postclassic period. This town, unlike other Maya sites, was not hidden away for centuries; the locals knew about it. However, it didn't gain fame until the 1800s, when European settlers began to investigate the area. Historians suspect Palenque was a business and religious hub due to the many ceremonial and bureaucratic buildings in the area (Roller 2022).[32] The palace at the site is probably the most impressive landmark.

---

[30] VanVoorst, Jenny Fretland. *The Ancient Maya*, 31–32.
[31] VanVoorst, Jenny Fretland. *The Ancient Maya*, 32–34.
[32] Roller, Sarah. "Lost Cities: A Victorian Explorer's Photos of Old Maya Ruins." Historyhit.com. History Hit,
February 24, 2022. https://www.historyhit.com/victorian-photos-of-maya-ruins/.

Palenque ruins.
https://pixabay.com/photos/mexico-palenque-ruins-maya-temple-3974404/

Tikal was also a major ceremonial and bureaucratic center. It is hard to say how far the city expanded, as its reach extended far outside the city itself. Government officials from the Maya capital of Tenochtitlan would often come there for business or religious purposes. Much of this site is still in ruins and covered with plant life. Because of this, the area has not been thoroughly investigated.[33] For these reasons, the city is most famous for what it was used for, rather than what it looks like.

Chichén Itzá was built sometime in the first half of the 5th century. Within the next one to two hundred years, Chichén Itzá became a large city, complete with suburbs. Historians guess that up to fifty thousand people lived there at its height, which was sometime between the 6th to the 13th centuries. Much of the land needed to be leveled in order to build on it. The Maya must have done a great job building structurally sound buildings, as a couple of them are still standing, including El Castillo and a government building in Las Monjas. The city also had paved roads, aqueducts, a spring, and a site

---

[33] Roller, Sarah. "Lost Cities: A Victorian Explorer's Photos of Old Maya Ruins."

for human sacrifices to take place. The city remained a busy business and religious hub until its decline in the 1500s.[34]

Pyramid of the Sun in Chichén Itzá.
https://pixabay.com/photos/chichen-itza-mexico-sun-weekend-1009113/

Logosyllabic Script

Even though the Maya was not the first Mesoamerican civilization to appear on the map, they *were* the first to come up with a single written language. This is impressive, not only because they were the first but because the Maya spoke more than one language but only had one written language. However, most people were illiterate; it is believed only the elite could read and write. This written language was made up of hieroglyphics. Some pictures represented whole words, while others represented syllables. All in all, the Maya are believed to have used about seven hundred unique symbols.[35] These symbols, like the Olmec written language, were similar to Egyptian hieroglyphics.

---

[34] History.com Editors. "Chichen Itza." History. A&E Television Networks, August 21, 2018.
Accessed May 20, 2022. https://www.history.com/topics/ancient-americas/chichen-itza.
[35] VanVoorst, Jenny Fretland. *The Ancient Maya*, 20–21.

Unfortunately, historians do not yet know how to read all of these symbols.

Possibly just as impressive as having a written language, the Maya also had a written system of numbers. What's so special about this is that the Maya had a number zero (0), which most ancient civilizations did not. Aside from the number zero, all of the numbers were represented by a series of dots or lines. Unlike the Arabic numbering system we use now, the Maya numbers had a base of twenty rather than ten.[36] The best part of all is that historians *do* know how to read their numbers. This makes deciphering documents much easier.

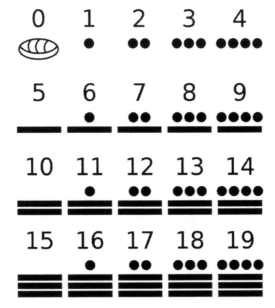

Maya numerals.
Neuromancer2K4 and Bryan Derk. CC-BY-SA 3.0, via Wikimedia.
https://commons.wikimedia.org/wiki/File:Maya.svg

---

[36] VanVoorst, Jenny Fretland. *The Ancient Maya*, 24.

Maya Calendar

Contrary to popular belief, the Maya had more than one calendar. Their most famous calendar is called the Haab. This calendar had 365 days in a year, the same as our current calendar. This showed that the Maya understood how long it took the Earth to fully revolve around the sun. However, they did not seem to account for leap days. For the most part, these calendars were used to plan the farming season and to schedule religious ceremonies.[37] It should be noted that the Haab calendar is *not* the calendar that people thought would predict the end of the world in 2012.

The "end-of-days" calendar, as we know it today, was the Long Count calendar. This calendar lasted 5,128 years in total. These types of calendars were used to mark the beginning and the end of ages. They were significant to kings and astronomers. While one calendar ended in 2012, that doesn't necessarily mean that the Maya thought the world would end in 2012, just that it would reach the end of the cycle.[38] This cycle was called a baktun. There were thirteen of these in total, with 2012 ending the thirteenth baktun. After this, the baktun would restart with the first.[39] However, people who did not understand Maya culture would see this as there being no new cycles. This explains why some people thought this meant the Maya were not preparing for any new years.

Astronomy

The Maya are famous for their interest in astronomy—the study of space, stars, and planets. Historians believe the Maya reached the peak of their interest in astronomy around 900 CE. The Maya believed that the stars and planets could teach them more about the gods. They used their findings to make calendars and even temples!

---

[37] VanVoorst, Jenny Fretland. *The Ancient Maya*, 25.
[38] VanVoorst, Jenny Fretland. *The Ancient Maya*, 26.
[39] "End of World in 2012? Maya "Doomsday" Calendar Explained." National Geographic. National Geographic, December 20, 2011. Accessed May 24, 2022. https://www.nationalgeographic.com/science/article/111220-end-of-world-2012-maya-calendar-explained-ancient-science.

The most important "planets" the Maya studied were the sun, moon, and Venus. Since the Maya did not have telescopes, it is not likely that they would have known much or anything about the other planets. Much of what they discovered was recorded in astronomical tables, usually written on temple walls. The one thing the Maya got wrong about astronomy is that they thought Earth was the center of the universe with all the other planets and the sun revolving around it. This was a common thought around the world at this time.[40] Even though historians and modern-day astronomers do not know how to read all of the Maya hieroglyphics, since the stars have more or less remained the same since the 900s, scientists can still fact-check what the Maya discovered. Shockingly, even without much technology, the Maya were right in a lot of their theories about astronomy!

Decline

Many history books will credit the end of the Maya civilization to the arrival of the Spanish conquistadors. While there is a lot of truth in this, the conquistadors were not the *only* cause for their decline. In fact, the Maya civilization began its decline centuries before the Spanish arrived.[41] The arrival of the Spanish, with their guns and diseases, was the final nail in the Maya's coffin.

Maya civilization peaked sometime around the 800 to 1000s CE. By this time, they had built many of their biggest temples, learned about astronomy, created a calendar, and conceived a written language. However, after this time period, more and more Maya (mostly commoners) began to move out of the cities in search of more fertile land. Historians think this may have been caused by droughts and other unfavorable farming conditions closer to the cities. Another cause could have been natural disasters, which would have encouraged people to move away from cities rather than trying to

---

[40] Minster, Christopher. "Ancient Maya Astronomy." ThoughtCo, July 24, 2019. https://www.thoughtco.com/ancient-maya-astronomy-2136314.
[41] VanVoorst, Jenny Fretland. *The Ancient Maya*, 36–39.

rebuild the cities.[42] Either way, this led to a major population decline in the cities.

When the Maya moved, they tended to head northward. This led to the building of many new cities. However, since there were *many* new cities, these cities tended to have lower populations than the southern cities. This, along with other factors, led to political instability, which made the cities anything but secure. By 1300, many of these new cities, including Chichén Itzá, were already abandoned.[43] This pattern would continue until the final piece of the puzzle clicked into place—the arrival of the Europeans.

The Spanish arrived in the "New World" around 1500 CE. They came in search of gold, glory, and God. At least, that's what they said. In reality, it was mostly for gold and glory—anything to do with God came later and usually as an afterthought. The Europeans didn't come empty-handed; they brought guns and diseases (including smallpox, typhus, and measles). Since these diseases were from Europe, the native peoples had no immunity to them. These diseases would end up killing more Maya than any Spanish gun ever did.[44] The same happened to Native Americans all over Mesoamerica and the surrounding areas.

By the mid-1500s, the Spanish, after having weakened the Maya significantly in previous decades, had control of about half of the Maya lands. During this time, the Spanish burned Maya books, destroyed artifacts, and tried to eliminate the Maya religion. This pattern continued until the late 1600s, when the Spanish had taken control of the last Maya city, effectively eliminating the Maya civilization.[45] However, the Spanish didn't kill *all* of the Maya. Some Spanish went on to marry and have children with the Maya. Because of this, the Maya still have living descendants to this day that carry on the culture, even if most of it has been lost to time and conquest.

---

[42] VanVoorst, Jenny Fretland. *The Ancient Maya*, 36–37.
[43] VanVoorst, Jenny Fretland. *The Ancient Maya*, 37.
[44] VanVoorst, Jenny Fretland. *The Ancient Maya*, 39.
[45] VanVoorst, Jenny Fretland. *The Ancient Maya*, 41.

The Maya Today

As of the 2000s, there are about six million people of Maya descent living in and around Central America. Many of these people also have Spanish heritage. Even with this intermixing, the Maya have retained many of their cultural traditions. However, many are now Christian (due to Spanish influence), so there is little to no worship of the old gods. Instead, most of the traditions they practice have more to do with agriculture, food, and the arts. Some Maya even know how to speak some of the ancient Maya languages![46] There is no saying how long the Maya traditions and culture will survive. No matter what, it is still impressive that they have managed to retain some of their traditions for this long.

---

[46] "The Maya Today." Canadian Museum of History. Canadian Museum of History, n.d. Accessed May 25, 2022.
https://www.historymuseum.ca/cmc/exhibitions/civil/maya/mmc08eng.html.

Chapter 3: The Terrific Toltecs

Considerably less is known about the Toltecs than the other Mesoamerican civilizations in this book. Most of the records historians have about this civilization come from the Aztecs and the Spanish. However, these records are often incomplete. Since the records were not written by the Toltecs, there is a chance that the records are biased and do not tell the stories from the Toltec point of view.[47] Much of what historians *do* have from the Toltecs directly comes from their artwork and architecture, which we will get into later in this chapter.

Compared to the other Mesoamerican civilizations, the Toltec civilization was relatively short-lived. It is difficult to say when exactly the Toltec civilization formed, as the people had roots in other tribes. With this in mind, historians guess that the Toltec civilization started sometime in the 900s CE with the settlement of Culhuacan. The Toltecs later moved and made their new capital in Tula (also known as Tollan).[48] The settlement was set up in much the same way as

---

[47] Cartwright, Mark. "Toltec Civilization." World History Encyclopedia. World History Publishing, April 27, 2018. https://www.worldhistory.org/Toltec_Civilization/.
[48] Cartwright, Mark. "Toltec Civilization."

Olmec and Maya cities, with temples and other pyramid-like buildings.

Origins

The Toltecs are likely descended, at least in part, from the Tolteca-Chichimeca people. They are also sometimes associated with the Nahua group. In the 800s CE, this tribe lived in modern-day northwestern Mexico but later migrated to the valley area of Mexico, where Culhuacan would later be settled. Legends say that the tribe was brought to the new area by their leader, Huemac. However, as he was a leader in the late 400s CE, this is not likely to have actually happened. Stories also say the Toltecs and Chichimeca fought in many battles for the land, but again, this may or may not have actually happened.[49] Then again, the Toltecs were warlike people, and much of their history is unclear, so it is impossible to say exactly how the civilization came to be.

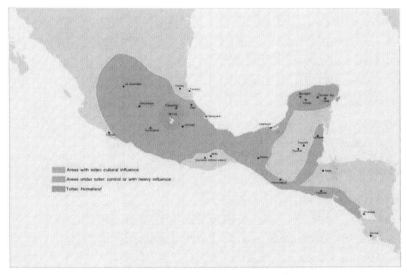

How far the Toltec influence spread.
Mabarlabin, CC BY-SA 3.0 https://creativecommons.org/licenses/by-sa/3.0 via Wikimedia Commons https://commons.wikimedia.org/wiki/File:Toltec_influence_cities_marked1.jpg

---

[49] Kessler, Peter. "Toltecs (Mesoamerica)." The History Files. Kessler Associates, n.d. https://www.historyfiles.co.uk/KingListsAmericas/CentralToltecs.htm.

Maya Influence

The Maya civilization predated the Toltec civilization by several hundred years and lasted several hundred years after the Toltec Empire turned to dust. Because of this, the Toltecs were able to both learn and take from the Maya while also growing up alongside them. The Maya also had an opportunity to learn and take from the Toltecs. With all of this going on at the same time, it can sometimes be difficult to know which culture borrowed from which originally.

The Toltecs took a lot of their city planning and architecture from the Maya. The Toltec capital of Tula was planned out similarly to the famous Maya city of Chichén Itzá.[50] It should be noted that this means that the street and city structure was similar. While the architecture did have many similarities, this was common for most Mesoamerican civilizations and was not a special representation of the Maya/Toltec bond.

Religion was another aspect of Maya culture the Toltecs took from and adapted to make it their own. Both religions have a feathered god spirit. This spirit is usually drawn as being part-human, part-bird. The Maya feathered spirit is Kukulcan, while the Toltec feathered spirit is Quetzalcoatl.[51] The Toltec and Maya had many other similar myths and gods; the comparison of Kukulcan and Quetzalcoatl is simply the most striking.

Religion

Like most Mesoamerican civilizations, the Toltec people were polytheistic. Their main god was Quetzalcoatl. Some of the other main gods included Tlaloc and Tezcatlipoca. Tlaloc was a rain god; he would have been important since much of Toltec life revolved around agriculture. Tezcatlipoca was Quetzalcoatl's brother and the god of the night sky. Some minor gods, who we do not know as much

---

[50] Cartwright, Mark. "Toltec Civilization."
[51] Cartwright, Mark. "Toltec Civilization."

about, include Centeotl and Xochiquetzal.[52] Similar to the Maya and Greek gods, the Toltec gods were imperfect and had many human traits. They were often represented as having animal body parts and traits, such as feathers or scales.

Human sacrifice was a grizzly part of the Toltec religion. The Toltecs even had several pieces of architecture dedicated to the practice, such as ball courts and temples. Sometimes, the human sacrifices were beheaded or had their hearts cut out. Heads would sometimes be put on display, while hearts and larger body parts might have been buried, burned, or stored in pottery. The popularity of human sacrifices depended on who was the current leader and high priest of the local area.[53] Much is written about human sacrifice, likely because it was so gruesome. However, just because it was written about often does not mean it was the Toltecs' primary way of worshiping the gods. It was likely used for special occasions rather than being an everyday event.

Ce Tecpatl Mixcoatl and Ce Acatl Topiltzin

Not much is known about Ce Tecpatl Mixcoatl, but what historians do know shows just how important this figure is to Toltec history. Ce Tecpatl Mixcoatl's story is a bit complicated, as he has both historical and mythological aspects to his life. Tradition says that Ce Tecpatl Mixcoatl led the early Toltecs to their new home and helped to found Culhuacan—the Toltecs' first big city and possibly first capital. He was deified after his death, becoming a sort of human-serpent god, and he was written about as a heroic warrior and leader with almost superhuman abilities.[54] He could be likened to a demigod and is often compared to Hercules.

---

[52] Minster, Christopher. "Overview of Toltec Gods and Religion." ThoughtCo, April 27, 2019.
https://www.thoughtco.com/toltec-gods-and-religion-2136271.
[53] Minster, Christopher. "Overview of Toltec Gods and Religion."
[54] Cartwright, Mark. "Toltec Civilization."

Significantly more is known about Ce Acatl Topiltzin, also known as Topiltzin Quetzalcoatl, than about his father. Like his father, he was a real person who was later deified. While his father had serpent-like traits, Topiltzin had bird-like traits, such as being covered with feathers. Part of the reason he became a bird-like spirit was because of his legendary crafting skills, which included featherwork. Another reason for this is a legend saying that Topiltzin sacrificed himself to the gods to save the city. He promised to return one day, similar to how Christians see Jesus.[55] For some reason, both of these early Toltec historical figures seem to be more revered in death than they were in life. This goes to show just how powerful Toltec religion and spirituality were.

Toltec Art and Architecture

The Toltecs did not leave much behind for us to learn from; most of what we know was left by the Aztecs, who mythologized much of the Toltecs' history. However, historians do have ancient artwork and architecture, which has been more or less untouched since the Toltec Empire was at its peak.

The Warrior Columns are probably some of the most famous Toltec sculptures. These are large statues that range in height, but they are usually taller than the average human. Most of these sculptures are made out of a single piece of stone. Many of them also have columns next to them, which are usually engraved with Toltec symbols and pictures. These usually have religious motifs as well.[56]

---

[55] Flood, Julia. "The Myth of Ce Acatl Topiltzin Quetzalcoatl." Mexicolore. Mexicolore, 2008. Accessed May 30, 2022, https://www.mexicolore.co.uk/aztecs/ask-us/ce-acatl-topiltzin-quetzalcoatl.
[56] Minster, Christopher. "Toltec Art, Sculpture and Architecture." ThoughtCo, April 24, 2018, https://www.thoughtco.com/toltec-art-sculpture-architecture-2136270.

An iconic collection of statues located on top of a pyramid in Tula. This group of statues is commonly known as the Atlanteans.
Arian Zwegers, CC-BY 2.0, via Flickr https://www.flickr.com/photos/azwegers/20660295926

Up next is the famous Chac Mool. This was a style of statue that was commonly used in religious ceremonies. These statues were carved out of one large piece of stone. However, they are not as tall as the Warrior Columns. Instead, they would be closer to the height of a table. The men carved in the statue held a small bowl. These bowls would be filled with sacrifices—sometimes human sacrifices[57]. Similar statues can also be found in **Maya** and **Aztec** ruins.

---

[57] Minster, Christopher. "Toltec Art, Sculpture and Architecture."

A Chac Mool from Chichén Itzá.
OliBac, CC-BY 2.0, via Flickr https://www.flickr.com/photos/olibac/4919280466

Last but not least is the Wall of Serpents. As the name implies, this isn't so much a statue as a relief carved into a stone wall. It is located in Tula. This may have been a religious carving, as snakes were important symbols in Toltec spirituality. The wall also shows snakes trying to eat humans.[58] Could this reference the importance of human sacrifice?

A part of the Serpent Wall.
Lgarciar, CC-SA 3.0, via Wikimedia
https://commons.wikimedia.org/wiki/File:Estela_del_Coatepantli.JPG

---

[58] Minster, Christopher. "Toltec Art, Sculpture and Architecture."

Decline

No one really knows why the Toltec civilization came to an end. All we know was that it was violent. The city of Tula was totally destroyed and possibly burned. However, historians don't know who did this or why they would have done it. It could have been a civil war, the Chichimeca tribe, or another local native group.[59] Historians do not know what happened to the Toltec people either. They could have dispersed or died when the city fell.

Influence

Some historians will say that the Toltecs took from the Aztec culture, while others will say that the Aztecs took from the Toltec culture. These two civilizations existed around the same time, with the Aztecs coming into power after the Toltec civilization had declined. So, it is likely that they learned from each other, with both of them taking and giving or inspiring parts of each other's cultures.

The early Aztecs would have made part of their land in the same area as the late Toltecs. Because of this link, some early Aztecs would claim to be descended from the Toltecs. Because they lived near the same area as the Toltecs, the Aztecs were able to see recent Toltec ruins. Not only did they draw inspiration from these ruins to build their own structures, but some Aztecs also took the artwork and other artifacts from Toltec sites to use as decorations.[60] While the Aztecs did take a lot, artistically and architecturally speaking, it is also likely that they came up with some ideas on their own or took them from other Mesoamerican cultures.

The Aztecs also borrowed the Toltecs' religious rites. The Toltecs are famous for being a warrior-fueled society. While some

---

[59] Minster, Christopher. "10 Facts About the Ancient Toltecs." ThoughtCo, August 27, 2019.
https://www.thoughtco.com/facts-about-the-ancient-toltecs-2136274.
[60] Vuckovic, Aleksa. "The Toltec Empire: Cultural Appropriation by the Aztecs?" Historic Mysteries. Net
Inceptions. 2021. Accessed May 26, 2022.
https://www.historicmysteries.com/toltec/.

contemporary writers may have exaggerated their violence, they didn't lie when they wrote about the Toltecs practicing human sacrifice to appease the gods. The Aztecs would later go on to do the same. The Aztecs even worshiped some of the same gods as the Toltecs, including one of their main gods, Quetzalcoatl.[61] It is also likely that the Aztecs borrowed other religious and cultural practices from the Toltecs, but these are some of the main examples.

---

[61] Vuckovic, Aleksa. "The Toltec Empire: Cultural Appropriation by the Aztecs?"

Chapter 4: The Amazing Aztecs

Even though the Aztecs were one of the most famous Mesoamerican native groups, they had one of the shortest-lived civilizations. They lasted about two hundred years, from 1325 to 1521 CE. Before the Aztecs were *the* Aztecs, they called themselves the Mexicas. They would later be known as the Aztecs since they emigrated from Aztlan. Legends say that they left their homeland because one of their gods, Huitzilopochtli, told them to. The Aztecs stopped traveling when they saw an eagle with a snake in its mouth sitting on top of a cactus. They took this as a sign that they had reached their new homeland. They settled in a new city called Tenochtitlan, which was on an island in modern-day Lake Texcoco.[62] The Aztecs would go on to cultivate the entire island and expand their empire from there.

---

[62] Dwyer, Helen and Stout, Mary. *Aztec History and Culture*, New York City, New York: Gareth Stevens Publishing, 2013, 10–12.

Painting of Tenochtitlan.
Gary Todd, CC-CC0, via Flickrhttps://www.flickr.com/photos/101561334@N08/9755215791/

However, there was a reason the island was empty. The land wasn't great for farming, and the surrounding tribes (which numbered almost fifty) knew it. To survive, the Aztecs had to make raised garden beds. Since the island was full of streams and other water sources, many of these gardens were floating or partially submerged in water. The Aztecs didn't discover this method of farming on their own but instead learned how to do this from the less famous Xochimilca tribe.[63] Because the Aztec tribe is more popular, they are still often credited with inventing this style of farming. In fact, if the Xochimilca tribe did not teach the Aztecs this, they either would have had to move, assimilate into another tribe, or die.

Alliance with Texcocans and Tacubans

One of the ways the Aztecs expanded their empire was by taking land from other tribes. While the Aztecs did have a strong group of warriors, their numbers were not big enough to conquer other tribes without help. Because of this, the Aztecs formed an alliance with both the Texcoco and Tlacopan tribes sometime in the mid-1400s.[64] Both these tribes and the Aztecs were eager to take more land for two main reasons: power and riches. As mentioned, there were about fifty other

---

[63] Roos, David. "How the Aztec Empire Was Forged Through a Triple Alliance." History. A&E TelevisionNetworks, February 24, 2021. https://www.history.com/news/aztec-empire-triple-alliance.

[64] Dwyer, Helen and Stout, Mary. *Aztec History and Culture*, 13.

tribes or city-states living in close proximity to the Aztecs. Out of these, the biggest and most powerful tribe in the early 1300s was the Azcapotzalco state, home of the Tepanec civilization. All new tribes to the area had to pay tribute to this tribe, which the Aztecs and their allies soon grew tired of.[65] Instead, they wanted the surrounding tribes to pay tribute to *them*. To understand how they would eventually accomplish this, we need to learn more about the leader who started the coup: Itzcoatl.

Itzcoatl

Itzcoatl, also known as the Obsidian Snake, was the *tlatoani* (king-like figure) of Tenochtitlan. At the beginning of his reign, he focused on his own people. However, in 1426, Azcapotzalco's *tlatoani* died. This left an open leadership space, and many other kings were willing to literally kill for it, Itzcoatl included. He was the one who encouraged the Aztecs to form their alliances with the Texcocans and Tlacopans.[66] Within a few years, the alliance controlled upward of twelve million people. The people who they conquered could either pay tribute to the alliance twice a year or face the consequences. While there was no set consequence for not paying tribute, the penalty was often death.[67] Itzcoatl would go on to reign until 1440.[68] His reign only ended because of his death.

Language and Writing

Like the Olmecs, the Aztecs spoke Nahuatl, a native Mesoamerican language. Because of this, they would have been able to easily communicate with other local tribes.[69] They also had a sort of written language that used pictograms, which was similar to hieroglyphics. They also used the same numbering system as the

---

[65] Roos, David. "How the Aztec Empire Was Forged Through a Triple Alliance."
[66] Roos, David. "How the Aztec Empire Was Forged Through a Triple Alliance."
[67] Dwyer, Helen and Stout, Mary. *Aztec History and Culture*, 13–14.
[68] Britannica, T. Editors of Encyclopedia. "Aztec." Encyclopedia Britannica, April 10, 2022. https://www.britannica.com/topic/Aztec.
[69] Britannica, T. Editors of Encyclopedia. "Aztec."

Maya.[70] This is impressive, as the Maya Empire died out hundreds of years before the Aztec Empire began.

Since the Aztecs had direct contact with the Spanish, the Spanish were able to write down how the Nahuatl language sounded by comparing it to Spanish pronunciations. While this didn't translate the language directly, it did help non-Aztecs know how the language was pronounced.[71] However, this did not help with the pictograms since they were more complicated to read.

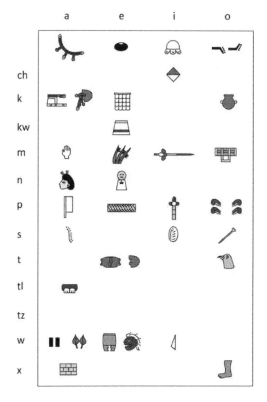

Aztec syllabary (According to Lacadena and Wichmann, 2004).
Paulo Calvo, CC-BY-SA 4.0, via Wikimedia,
https://commons.wikimedia.org/wiki/File:Aztec_silabary_in_IPA_Lacadena_Wichmann_2004.jpg

---

[70] "Aztec System of Writing: Pictograms." History on the Net. Salem Media, May 31, 2022
https://www.historyonthenet.com/aztec-system-of-writing-pictograms.
[71] Britannica, T. Editors of Encyclopedia. "Aztec."

Religion

When it comes to religion, the Aztecs borrowed a lot from other Mesoamerican civilizations, mostly from the Maya and Toltecs. The Aztecs were polytheistic. They had not only many gods but also many heavens and underworlds. Some of the main gods included Tonatiuh (the sun god), Tlaloc (the rain god), Huitzilopochtli (the war god), and Quetzalcoatl (the feathered serpent).[72] Remember, Quetzalcoatl was a part historical, part godlike figure the Toltecs also revered.

Giving offerings was an important part of Aztec religion. Sometimes, human hearts were offered to the gods. This would usually involve a human sacrifice. Most of the human sacrifices were prisoners of war from neighboring tribes. The Aztecs also sometimes sacrificed blood; this could be done by bloodletting and didn't necessarily require a death.[73] Like most religions, the Aztec religion also had holidays and other celebrations. Aztecs often had ceremonies involving sacrifices on these festive days.

Daily Life

Aztec society was broken up into three basic parts. The part of society a person occupied would determine just about everything they could do, from what they could eat to what they could wear. For the most part, a person could not change their position in society. The highest level included the royalty, nobles, military leaders, and landowners. Religious leaders may have also been in this grouping. The middle class contained artisans and merchants. The next class (the commoners) had the most people. These were the laborers, farmers, and soldiers. Slaves were at the very bottom. They were most often criminals or war captives.[74] This sort of class system was common in most early civilizations around the world.

Both boys and girls were able to attend school, starting around age seven. The schools were divided up by social class rather than by

---

[72] Britannica, T. Editors of Encyclopedia. "Aztec."
[73] Britannica, T. Editors of Encyclopedia. "Aztec."
[74] Dwyer, Helen and Stout, Mary. *Aztec History and Culture*, 20–21.

gender. School would end sometime around age fourteen to twenty. Girls usually finished school earlier since they were able to get married as teenagers. Men usually waited until their late teens or early twenties to get married.[75] It is not clear whether or not the Aztecs married for love or had arranged marriages. Most married couples would go on to have children. It is also not clear if sex before marriage was allowed or was a social taboo.

Architecture

Like with many other aspects of Aztec culture, the Aztecs took a lot of their building methods and styles from the Maya and Toltecs. Of course, the Aztecs added details to help make their buildings unique. The main city, where most of the old architecture has been found, was Tenochtitlan. Here, there were temples, plazas, ball courts, shrines, and government buildings. Commoner and merchant houses would be outside of the main city, like a modern-day suburb.[76] Today, the temples and ball courts are some of the most popular tourist destinations in Mexico.

View from Pyramid of the Moon, Tenochtitlan.
MollySVH, CC-BY 2.0, Flickr https://www.flickr.com/photos/18472724@N00/3365451381

---

[75] Dwyer, Helen and Stout, Mary. *Aztec History and Culture*, 22–23.
[76] "Aztec Architecture." Legends & Chronicles. Legends and Chronicles, accessed May 31, 2022, https://www.legendsandchronicles.com/ancient-civilizations/the-ancient-aztecs/aztec-architecture/.

Outside of their stonework architecture, the Aztecs are best-known for their floating gardens, also called chinampas. These floating patches of agricultural land were usually only a couple of meters wide but could be up to thirty meters long. The chinampas were naturally irrigated since they were surrounded by canals. They were also often divided by tree roots. Generally, these were located outside of the living "suburb" area.[77] Chinampas are still used today in some parts of Central and South America.

Montezuma II

There were several leaders between Itzcoatl and Montezuma II. During this time, the Aztec Empire continued to rise to power. However, Montezuma II stands out as a ruler. He was the last long-serving Aztec king; his successors would last less than a year each. Montezuma began his reign in 1502. At the start of his reign, the Aztec Empire spread from modern-day Nicaragua to Honduras. While the territory was large, it was weak. Infighting and other political conflicts made the Aztecs easy bait for any challengers, which the Spanish would take advantage of.[78] If the Aztec civilization was not so weakened, then the Spanish might not have been able to conquer them. At the very least, it would have taken the Spanish much longer to conquer them.

Of course, Montezuma wasn't going to give the Aztec Empire up without a fight. He tried to bribe Hernán Cortés, a Spanish conquistador, to leave. However, Cortés had already made alliances with other native tribes who had a bone to pick with the Aztecs. In time, Cortés was able to capture Montezuma and keep him prisoner. Montezuma II would die a few days after being captured on June 30th,

---

[77] "Aztec Architecture." Legends & Chronicles.

[78] Britannica, T. Editors of Encyclopedia. "Montezuma II." *Encyclopedia Britannica*, April 20, 2022.
https://www.britannica.com/biography/Montezuma-II.

1520.[79] His death would only be the beginning of the Aztec Empire's downfall.

Downfall

The Spanish, namely the Spanish conquistadors, was the final nail in the coffin for the Aztec Empire. As mentioned, the empire was already weakened due to infighting, and the Spanish only made things worse. Hernán Cortés and about five hundred other Europeans under his command met the Aztecs in 1519. Not only did the Europeans bring new foods, animals, and weapons, but they also brought diseases.[80] Since the diseases were new to Mexico, the Aztecs did not have any natural immunity to them. There were also no vaccines at this time, which meant that many Aztecs would die without the Spanish firing a single bullet.

At first, the Spanish were welcomed with open arms. It is widely believed that Montezuma II had originally mistaken Cortés as a god. This belief wouldn't last for long, as the Spanish soon allied themselves with tribes that hated the Aztecs. They invaded, which would kick off a two-year war. Finally, on August 13th, 1521, the Spanish took Tenochtitlan. This ended the Aztec rule and civilization.[81] However, the Aztecs were not all murdered. They still have living descendants today, as many Aztecs went on to have children with Europeans.

Influence Today

Most, if not all, people of Aztec descent also have Spanish blood running through their veins. With this in mind, it makes perfect sense that the current Aztec culture would be a blend of the traditional Aztec ways and Spanish influence. Today, they mainly live in Guerrero and Hidalgo, Mexico. Some also live in northern Mexico and southern California.[82] Unlike some North American Native

---

[79] Britannica, T. Editors of Encyclopedia. "Montezuma II."
[80] Britannica, T. Editors of Encyclopedia. "Aztec."
[81] Britannica, T. Editors of Encyclopedia. "Aztec."
[82] Dwyer, Helen and Stout, Mary. *Aztec History and Culture*, 31.

Americans, the Aztecs were not given reservations to move to but instead had to acclimate to Spanish culture.

Some of the people descended from Aztecs, now called the Nahuas, can still speak the ancient Nahuatl language. In the 2010s, about a million people in Mexico could speak Nahuatl. However, only two-thirds of these people can read and write in this language.[83] Most Mexicans and Nahuas use Spanish as their primary language.

The Spanish did change a lot about the Aztec culture. One of the first things the Spanish did was destroy temples and dismantle the government. The Aztecs were forced to convert to Catholicism, and images of the old gods were destroyed or forgotten. Today, most Nahuas are still Catholic, although they do uphold some ancient beliefs, such as praying to spirits.[84] There is no set Nahuas religion today. Instead, it is up to each person to decide how they worship.

---

[83] Dwyer, Helen and Stout, Mary. *Aztec History and Culture*, 31–32.
[84] Dwyer, Helen and Stout, Mary. *Aztec History and Culture*, 33–34.

Chapter 5: The Incredible Incas

The Inca Empire first appeared on the map around 1100 CE, first living in and around the Andes Mountains. The Incas called their country Tawantinsuyu, but for the purpose of this chapter, we will refer to all Inca-controlled land as the Inca Empire. Their first capital was Cusco (also spelled Cuzco). Like the Aztecs, the Spanish would cause the end of the Inca Empire in the 1500s. During the Inca Empire, the Maya Empire came to an end, and the Aztec Empire both started and ended.[85] However, the Incas were not in Mesoamerica; it is the only civilization in our book that was not. In the past, though, they were often lumped together with the other Mesoamerican civilizations. However, the Incas were the largest pre-Columbian civilization in the Americas, which warrants a closer look at their empire.

Taking Land

The Incas expanded their empire as most empires do: by taking land from other neighboring tribes and empires. However, the Incas didn't do this as soon as they formed their empire. Instead, the Incas waited until about 1400 CE to start taking land. Part of the reason the

---

[85] History.com Editors. "Inca." History. A&E Television Networks, March 11, 2015. Accessed June 1, 2022.
https://www.history.com/topics/south-america/inca.

empire was not expanding before this was that they were building up not only the base of their empire but also their military.[86] This would prepare them for what was about to happen and aid them in taking land when it mattered most.

The Chanca (or Chanka) tribe provoked the Incas into engaging in their first major battle with another tribe in 1438. During this battle, the Incas were able to defend their own lands and take Chanca land, which allowed the Incas to expand their empire to the Titicaca Basin in the south. In the following years, the Incas would expand their empire northward, taking land from the Cajamarca and Chima tribes.[87] As the decades rolled on, the Incas continued to take more and more land, which also meant taking control of more and more native peoples.

By about 1500, the Inca Empire had spread so far that it contained about twelve million people, who were a part of over one hundred ethnic groups. All of these people were considered to be under Inca control, but they likely retained parts of their original cultures before slowly acclimating over the decades. The Incas connected all of their lands with roadways, which would have likely been dirt trails. The Incas would use these trails for trade and to collect taxes. After all, it was the tax money and goods (usually food) that helped to fund the trails to begin with.[88]

---

[86] History.com Editors. "Inca."
[87] History.com Editors. "Inca."
[88] History.com Editors. "Inca."

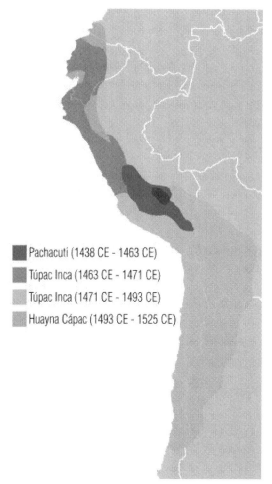

Inca expansion (1438-1533).
QQuantum, CC-BY-SA 4.0, Via Wikimedia
https://commons.wikimedia.org/wiki/File:Inca_Expansion.svg

Pachacuti Inca Yupanqui

While there were at least a dozen Inca emperors, some were more important than others. One of the most important of these emperors was Pachacuti Inca Yupanqui, also known as Pachacutec. He was the ninth Inca emperor, and he reigned from 1438 to 1471. Pachacutec is most famous for conquering other tribes' lands and greatly expanding the Inca Empire. However, he did not make the biggest expansion;

rather, his expansion was important because it was the first major expansion the Inca Empire had done.[89]

Topa Inca Yupanqui

Topa Inca Yupanqui, also known by the first names Thupa and Túpac, was the tenth Inca emperor. He gained the throne after Pachacuti abdicated the throne in 1471. Since this acted more as a retirement than anything else, the transition of power was peaceful. However, Topa's rule was anything *but* peaceful. Shortly after claiming the throne, the Colla and Lupaca tribes started a rebellion against the Inca Empire. The Inca military went after Colla first, attacking them near Pucará. Next, they moved to fight the Lupaca in the Titicaca Basin. However, fighting the Colla first gave the Lupaca time to ally themselves with the Pacasa. Even this extra help couldn't match the Inca army, and the rebellious tribes were soon defeated.[90] This fighting would have taken place in jungles and on mountains, making the battles especially dangerous and difficult.

During the next several years, Topa would lead the Inca Empire, claiming many new lands in the process. By 1476, the Incas held most of the area in and around the Andes Mountains. However, Topa still wanted more land for his empire. Next, he took his army to the Cañete Valley to take lands from the native there. The war took three years, but the Incas finally managed to take more land in what is now Peru. He then continued to take land until his death in 1493.[91] Topa took more land than any other Inca emperor, more than doubling the size of the empire.

---

[89] Britannica, T. Editors of Encyclopedia. "Pachacuti Inca Yupanqui." *Encyclopedia Britannica*, June 24, 2019.
https://www.britannica.com/biography/Pachacuti-Inca-Yupanqui.
[90] Sanders, W. T., Soustelle, Jacques, Bushnell, Geoffrey H. S., Hagen, Victor Wolfgang von, Murra, John V.,
Patterson, Thomas C., Willey, Gordon R. and Coe, Michael Douglas. "Pre-Columbian civilizations." Encyclopedia Britannica, November 18, 2020.
https://www.britannica.com/topic/pre-Columbian-civilizations.
[91] Sanders et al. "Pre-Columbian civilizations."

Religion

Like all of the other civilizations in this book, the Incas were also polytheistic. Their religion was a mixture of animism and worshiping gods that controlled various aspects of nature. Their main god was Inti, the sun god. Worship of the sun god was part of the empire-wide state religion. People living in the Inca Empire could also choose to worship other gods as well. Some of the other popular Inca gods included Viracocha, the creator god; Apu Illapu, the rain and agriculture god; and Mama Quilla, the sun god's wife and the goddess of the moon and femininity.[92] Some of these gods went by other names as well.

Architecture

Even though the Inca Empire came to an end about five hundred years ago, many of its temples still stand tall. Even some traces of paint remain on temple walls! The ruins are absolutely beautiful and have held up considerably better than the Mesoamerican buildings from this time period. Part of the reason for this is because the limestone rocks used to build many of the Inca structures were quarried and squared off so the stones could link in with each other. The Incas did not need to use mortar since the stones were cut to fit perfectly together. Once the walls were stacked, construction workers sanded the edges, making the blocks smoother.[93] Of course, doing such precise and labor-intensive work would have been very expensive. This style was mostly saved for public, holy, and government buildings.

The average house and other "cheaper" buildings were more often than not built with local stones that had not been quarried or cut. These were stacked on top of each other and held in place with a muddy or clay-like mortar. Once all of the blocks were in place,

---

[92] Murra, J. V. and Hagen, Victor Wolfgang von. "Inca religion." Encyclopedia Britannica, March 17, 2021. https://www.britannica.com/topic/Inca-religion.
[93] Cartwright, Mark. "Inca Architecture." World History Encyclopedia. World History Publishing Last modified

another layer of mortar would be added and smoothed out. This makes for the classic adobe house style. Sometimes, the structures were built right into the mountainside! The roofs could also be made out of stone, but they were more often made from trees, branches, leaves, and reeds. The Incas were famous for using the landscape to help with their constructions.[94] Since all of these roofing materials were biodegradable, they are no longer on the structures. Because of this, the houses look like they were built without a roof.

Cusco

The area of and surrounding Cusco has been occupied since 500 BCE, mostly by the Chanapata civilization. The Inca didn't come into the area until about 1200 CE. It officially became the capital of the Inca Empire when Manco Capac was the emperor, sometime during the 1300s CE. By 1400, the Incas had begun to expand to other areas, keeping Cusco as their capital.[95] With such a long occupation, many tribes contributed to the city's layout and architecture. Even though the Incas were there for a relatively short amount of time, they arguably had the biggest impact on Cusco.

March 13, 2014. https://www.worldhistory.org/Inca_Architecture/.
[94] Cartwright, Mark. "Inca Architecture."
[95] Cartwright, Mark. "Cuzco." World History Encyclopedia. World History Publishing, January 30, 2015.

The ruins of Cusco, Peru.
Luis Vivanco, Pixabay License, Pixabay https://pixabay.com/illustrations/cusco-incas-peru-peruvian-ancient-2422267/

At Cusco's peak (between 1400 and 1500), the city could have held up to 150,000 people comfortably. However, most of the city was set up to accommodate temples and government buildings rather than humble dwellings. Nobles and other higher-ups would have been the city's primary occupants. Some of the most impressive buildings in Cusco include the Terrace of Repose and the Fortunate Terrace. These buildings, among others, would have been decorated with bas reliefs, gems, stones, and colorful paints.[96]

---

[96] Cartwright, Mark. "Cuzco."

Circular terraces in Cusco.
Teo Romera, CC-BY-SA 2.0, Flickr https://www.flickr.com/photos/teosaurio/4533134472

Machu Picchu

Machu Picchu is one of the Inca Empire's most famous sites; it was also one of the last cities the Incas built. Historians think the city, which stretches about five miles, was built sometime during the 1400 or 1500s. However, it was not inhabited for very long. The Incas left this settlement only about one hundred years after they built it. This was not due to the Spanish conquest but possibly because of the smallpox disease the Spanish spread.[97] Because the Spanish never attacked Machu Picchu, the city's ruins are more preserved than most other Inca and Mesoamerican sites.

---

[97] History.com Editors. "Machu Picchu." History. A&E Television Networks. June 13, 2011. Accessed June 3,
2022. https://www.history.com/topics/south-america/machu-picchu.

Machu Picchu.
4758892, Pixabay License, Pixabay https://pixabay.com/photos/peru-mountains-machu-picchu-2135770/

Historians and architects cannot agree on what Machu Picchu may have been used for. Some argued that it was a place for royalty and nobles to live, while others think it was a religious site. Other guesses include Machu Picchu being a trading center, a sort of school or place to study, or even a jail.[98] Even though we do not know what the purpose of Machu Picchu was, we do know that it was intricately designed and beautiful. This makes it a great tourist destination today.

Decline

Just like the Aztecs, the decline of the Inca Empire was directly influenced by the arrival of the Spanish. The first weapon the Spanish used, whether unknowingly or not, was smallpox. This disease took out both the Inca leader, Huayna Capac, and his successor. The death of both of these men left a hole in the government. Who would be the next Inca emperor? A civil war broke out over this issue, which

---

[98] History.com Editors. "Machu Picchu."

would only further weaken the Inca Empire.[99] All of these factors would only make it easier for the Spanish to conquer the Incas.

Francisco Pizarro would be the death of the Inca Empire and the king, Atahualpa. He kidnapped the king in 1532 and killed him a few months later. A few months after that, in late 1533, the Spanish took Cusco and installed a new puppet king, Manco Inca Yupanqui, to do their bidding. However, the Incas went on to rebel against the Spanish in 1536; they soon lost that battle. Various other battles between the Spanish and Incas continued until 1572, when the Spanish finally claimed victory, ending the Inca Empire for good.[100] Many of the Incas would go on to marry and have children with the Spanish, similar to what the Aztecs did. By doing this, part of the Inca culture lives on today.

Influence

Since the Incas left behind no written records, all of their cultural stories and traditions had to be carried down orally through families and communities. Despite that, the Inca culture has survived relatively well, especially in Peru. Today, 45 percent of people living in Peru have some Inca ancestry! Most of these people are rural farmers and live in tight-knit communities with other Inca descendants. For the most part, they all speak Quechua and are Roman Catholic, but they might worship some traditional Inca spirits.[101] These facts may not apply to all Inca descendants but instead should be used as a generalization.

---

[99] History.com Editors. "Inca."
[100] History.com Editors. "Inca."
[101] Murra, J. V. and Hagen, Victor Wolfgang von. "Inca religion." Encyclopedia Britannica, March 17, 2021. https://www.britannica.com/topic/Inca-religion.

Conclusion

The various Mesoamerican native civilizations defined the early centuries of Mexico. Without them, there's no saying what the country would be like now, only that it would be vastly different. And the Incas, of course, greatly influenced South America. All of the civilizations discussed in this book helped to create the first large cities and roadways that later generations would build on to make modern cities. Today, the city of Cusco still thrives and has native descendants living on every block.

Not only did most of these civilizations impact modern-day Mexico, but they also impacted each other. How would the Aztecs have prospered if it hadn't been for everything they had learned from the Toltecs? From learning how to create floating gardens to using well-traveled trade routes, these civilizations depended on each other, even if some were separated by centuries. The newer civilizations all had something to learn from the older, and this shows itself in many ways: art, architecture, religion, and customs.

As time goes on, it is likely that historians and archaeologists will discover more about these ancient civilizations, which will no doubt bring light to the life of Central and South America. Maybe one day, we will be able to read ancient pictographs like we can read Egyptian hieroglyphics. Either way, there is always more to learn about these civilizations. Hopefully, this short introduction to these cultures helped to spark an interest. We encourage you to learn more about these great civilizations so their history can be passed down for many generations to come.

Here's another book by Enthralling History that you might like

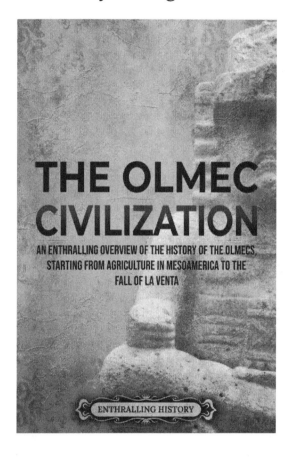

Free limited time bonus

Stop for a moment. We have a free bonus set up for you. The problem is this: we forget 90% of everything that we read after 7 days. Crazy fact, right? Here's the solution: we've created a printable, 1-page pdf summary for this book that you're reading now. All you have to do to get your free pdf summary is to go to the following website: **https://livetolearn.lpages.co/enthrallinghistory/**

Once you do, it will be intuitive. Enjoy, and thank you!

Bibliography

"Aztec Architecture." Legends & Chronicles. Legends and Chronicles, accessed May 31, 2022, https://www.legendsandchronicles.com/ancient-civilizations/the-ancient-aztecs/aztec-architecture/.

"Aztec System of Writing: Pictograms." History on the Net. Salem Media, May 31, 2022 https://www.historyonthenet.com/aztec-system-of-writing-pictograms.

Britannica, T. Editors of Encyclopedia. "Aztec." Encyclopedia Britannica, April 10, 2022. https://www.britannica.com/topic/Aztec

Britannica, T. Editors of Encyclopedia. "Inca." *Encyclopedia Britannica*, September 21, 2021. https://www.britannica.com/topic/Inca

Britannica, T. Editors of Encyclopedia. "Montezuma II." *Encyclopedia Britannica*, April 20, 2022. https://www.britannica.com/biography/Montezuma-II

Britannica, T. Editors of Encyclopedia. "Pachacuti Inca Yupanqui." *Encyclopedia Britannica*, June 24, 2019. https://www.britannica.com/biography/Pachacuti-Inca-Yupanqui

Cartwright, Mark. "Coyolxauhqui >> Mixcoatl >> Ancient Origins" Wiki Didactic. Edukalife, February 11, 2016.

https://edukalife.blogspot.com/2015/08/ancient-agriculture-origins-and-history.html

Cartwright, Mark. "Cuzco." World History Encyclopedia. World History Publishing, January 30, 2015, https://www.worldhistory.org/Cuzco/.

Cartwright, Mark. "Inca Architecture." World History Encyclopedia. World History Publishing Last modified March 13, 2014.

https://www.worldhistory.org/Inca_Architecture/.

Cartwright, Mark. "Toltec Civilization." World History Encyclopedia. World History Publishing, April 27, 2018. https://www.worldhistory.org/Toltec_Civilization/.

Dwyer, Helen and Stout, Mary. *Aztec History and Culture*, New York City, New York: Gareth Stevens Publishing, 2013.

"Early Classic Period (100–600 CE)." Encyclopedia Britannica. Encyclopedia Britannica, inc. Accessed May 18, 2022. https://www.britannica.com/topic/pre-Columbian-civilizations/Early-Classic-period-100-600-ce.

"End of World in 2012? Maya "Doomsday" Calendar Explained." National Geographic. National Geographic, December 20, 2011. Accessed May 24, 2022.

https://www.nationalgeographic.com/science/article/111220-end-of-world-2012-maya-calendar-explained-ancient-science.

Flood, Julia. "The Myth of Ce Acatl Topiltzin Quetzalcoatl." Mexicolore. Mexicolore, 2008. Accessed May 30, 2022, https://www.mexicolore.co.uk/aztecs/ask-us/ce-acatl-topiltzin-quetzalcoatl.

Heath, Haiden. "Has the Olmec Language Been Deciphered?" Rampfesthudson.com. Rampfest Hudson, October 25, 2019. https://www.rampfesthudson.com/has-the-olmec-language-been-deciphered/.

History.com Editors. "Chichen Itza." History. A&E Television Networks, August 21, 2018. Accessed May 20, 2022. https://www.history.com/topics/ancient-americas/chichen-itza

History.com Editors. "Inca." History. A&E Television Networks, March 11, 2015. Accessed June 1, 2022. https://www.history.com/topics/south-america/inca

History.com Editors. "Machu Picchu." History. A&E Television Networks. June 13, 2011. Accessed June 3, 2022. https://www.history.com/topics/south-america/machu-picchu

Kessler, Peter. "Toltecs (Mesoamerica)." The History Files. Kessler Associates, n.d. https://www.historyfiles.co.uk/KingListsAmericas/CentralToltecs.htm

"Maya Criminal Law." Tarlton Law Library. The University of Texas at Austin, November 8, 2018. https://tarlton.law.utexas.edu/aztec-and-maya-law/maya-criminal-law

"Maya Political Structure." Tarlton Law Library. The University of Texas at Austin, November 8, 2018. https://tarlton.law.utexas.edu/aztec-and-maya-law/maya-political-structure

Minster, Christopher. "10 Facts About the Ancient Toltecs." ThoughtCo, August 27, 2019. https://www.thoughtco.com/facts-about-the-ancient-toltecs-2136274

Minster, Christopher. "Ancient Maya Astronomy." ThoughtCo, July 24, 2019.
https://www.thoughtco.com/ancient-maya-astronomy-2136314

Minster, Christopher. "Ancient Olmec Culture." ThoughtCo, May 30, 2019.
https://www.thoughtco.com/olmec-culture-overview-2136299

(accessed May 17, 2022).

Minster, Christopher. "Economy and Trade of the Ancient Mayas." ThoughtCo, April 24, 2021. https://www.thoughtco.com/ancient-maya-economy-and-trade-2136168

https://www.thoughtco.com/ancient-maya-economy-and-trade-2136168 (accessed May 18, 2022).

Minster, Christopher. "Overview of Toltec Gods and Religion." ThoughtCo, April 27, 2019. https://www.thoughtco.com/toltec-gods-and-religion-2136271

Minster, Christopher. "The Historic Olmec City of San Lorenzo." ThoughtCo, June 15, 2019. https://www.thoughtco.com/the-olmec-city-of-san-lorenzo-2136302 (accessed May 17, 2022).

Minster, Christopher. "Toltec Art, Sculpture and Architecture." ThoughtCo, April 24, 2018, https://www.thoughtco.com/toltec-art-sculpture-architecture-2136270.

Murra, J. V. and Hagen, Victor Wolfgang von. "Inca religion." Encyclopedia Britannica, March 17, 2021.https://www.britannica.com/topic/Inca-religion

Roller, Sarah. "Lost Cities: A Victorian Explorer's Photos of Old Maya Ruins." Historyhit.com. History Hit, February 24, 2022.

https://www.historyhit.com/victorian-photos-of-maya-ruins

Roos, David. "How the Aztec Empire Was Forged Through a Triple Alliance." History. A&E Television Networks, February 24, 2021.

https://www.history.com/news/aztec-empire-triple-alliance

Sanders, W. T., Soustelle, Jacques, Bushnell, Geoffrey H. S., Hagen, Victor Wolfgang von, Murra, John V., Patterson, Thomas C., Willey, Gordon R. and Coe, Michael Douglas. "Pre-Columbian civilizations." Encyclopedia Britannica, November 18, 2020.

https://www.britannica.com/topic/pre-Columbian-civilizations

Scheper, George L. "The Olmec World." Academia.edu. Academia, October 1, 2014.

https://www.academia.edu/8578552/The_Olmec_World_or_the_Formative_Era_Ceremonial_Complex_Draft_Text_Copy_2

"The Maya Today." Canadian Museum of History. Canadian Museum of History, n.d. Accessed May 25, 2022.

https://www.historymuseum.ca/cmc/exhibitions/civil/maya/mmc08eng.html

"The Olmec | Ancient Civilizations (Article)." Khan Academy. Khan Academy, 2017.

https://www.khanacademy.org/humanities/world-history/world-history-beginnings/ancient-americas/a/the-olmec-article

VanVoorst, Jenny Fretland. *The Ancient Maya.* North Mankato, MN: Compass Point Books, 2013.

Vuckovic, Aleksa. "The Toltec Empire: Cultural Appropriation by the Aztecs?" Historic Mysteries. Net Inceptions. 2021. Accessed May 26, 2022.

https://www.historicmysteries.com/toltec

World History Encyclopedia. "Olmec Civilization Timeline." World History Encyclopedia RSS, 2022.
https://www.worldhistory.org/timeline/Olmec_Civilization

Made in the USA
Middletown, DE
19 July 2024

57637371R00040